The Community-Building College:

Leading the Way to Community Revitalization

Ervin L. Harlacher
&
James F. Gollattscheck

Published by the Community College Press, a division of the
American Association of Community Colleges
One Dupont Circle, NW, Suite 410
Washington,DC 20036
202/728-0200

ISBN 0-87117-297-6

Abstract

IT IS AN OVER-SIMPLIFICATION TO CLAIM THAT EDUCATION IS THE ANSWER to the needs of America's communities. As presently organized and delivered, education is irrelevant to the needs and aspirations of all too many. America's communities, buffeted by unprecedented change, require a future-oriented education, delivered through a flexible learning system that allows everyone, at any time, to learn as their needs dictate. It must be a system that achieves efficiency through partnerships and effectiveness through continuous evaluation, and which harnesses the very technology that now drives constant societal change to solve our nation's most pressing needs through the creation of learning communities.

Table of Contents

Foreword

A New Golden Age

DESPITE SEEMINGLY INSURMOUNTABLE PROBLEMS, A NEW MILLENNIUM offers all Americans great hope and promise. The disarray felt in so many communities can be overcome, and we can realize a revitalized national spirit. But all of our hopes depend upon a radical reconceptualization of education. Simply put, we cannot rely on an educational system designed by an agricultural society that prized punctuality, obedience, rote work, and linear thinking. The key to human survival in the dawning millennium is the reorganization of education around such concepts as lifelong learning, the empowerment of self-directed learners, and the creation of learning communities (Knowles, 1989, p. ix). Education must become a lifespan process.

This call for lifespan learning poses an especially great challenge for community college trustees, administrators and faculty. While others must share in this work, the responsibility for leading this effort will fall to the community college. After all, the community college was invented to help solve problems. In mid-century, locally created community colleges met the needs of veterans in their own home towns. More recently, when technological advances threatened America's global competitiveness, community colleges helped to re-skill the nation's workforce and lay the foundation for renewed economic growth.

But community colleges cannot rest on past accomplishments. Their future depends on their success in meeting the challenge of **building learning communities**. For those community colleges willing to make such a transformation, this work offers both a vision of the 21st learning community and a blueprint to guide community colleges and their communities in this vital undertaking.

While nothing we propose will be easily accomplished, we nevertheless share Teachers College president Arthur Levine's optimistic view of the future, offered at the 1995 Annual Convention of the American Association of Community Colleges (AACC):

> We are living through a very difficult time. And that's the hard news. But the good news, the very exciting news, is that no generation has had a chance to put its seal, its mark on higher education the way that we do. This is without question an incredibly exciting era to be living through.

PART I

Creating a Vision for a New Century

MUCH HAS BEEN SAID ABOUT THE CHALLENGES OF THE 21ST CENTURY. And many of the predictions share a deep sense of our collective disillusionment. Do we not all feel that ours is a nation in which everything seems to be broken—government, business, health care, and especially education (Levine, 1995)?

At the root of this unease with the future is our common experience of profound and constant change. Change has not only touched us individually, it has undermined our confidence in the effectiveness of public policy and the institutions that carry out that policy. Who, any longer, believes that our institutions, and especially our schools, can eliminate social ills? Can any program end poverty or crime, or bring health care within the reach of us all? It is no wonder that Sheldon Hackney (1995) sees an America "withdrawn from the public square."

Some argue that this dissolution of community, as Americans have known it for more than 200 years, is now irreversible. *This is not our view*. We retain a basic optimism in the capacity of our communities to empower and renew themselves. And we believe firmly that the community college can lead this renewal.

But what strategies should a community college adopt that can build consensus among the diverse elements of our communities on the direction this renewal should take? As a guide for those ready to take up this challenge, this work offers both a vision of the future and the tools to achieve this vision. Our vision begins with education. We agree with former US Secretary of Education Terrel H. Bell (1991) that education will remain the key to solving many of the problems in our society—from the need for greater productivity on the assembly line to a reduction in unemployment (p. 2).

However, we are not speaking of education in a traditional, narrow sense. For us, education is the process of facilitating growth, of bringing change and improvement to the lives of people. But our vision does not end with the individual. It extends to the community itself, to the building of **learning communities.** We see 21st century America as a web of learning communities, all committed to empowering individuals to function proficiently in a world of accelerating change. And we see America's community colleges, in partnership with other community organizations, taking the lead in planning for and implementing learning communities.

If America's communities are to be reborn, education must become nothing less than an essential public utility. It must permeate the entire community. It must empower people to learn, at their own rate and on their own time schedule, in multiple ways and at convenient sites, and at a cost they can afford. Through a renewed system of education, we must become a nation of open and dynamic learning communities.

CHAPTER I

Our Vision of the Learning Community

OUR VISION OF THE LEARNING COMMUNITY IS SIMPLE. IT IS THE SUP-portive context that empowers each of us to learn what we need to know, at any time, and in any place. It is a collaborative effort that unites local educational providers and is spearheaded by the community college. The learning community will be efficient, because of its reliance on technology. It will also be effective, because it monitors itself through rigorous community-needs assessment and program measurement. The learning community will also prepare each of us to respond to new situations, by encouraging initiative and the acquisition of new skills, attitudes, and values (Botkin, 1979, p. 8). It will teach *everyone* how to live meaningfully, to feel and understand, to act with intelligence, and to resolve issues and problems. In the learning community philosophy and commitment will override structure.

And most importantly, where education is now the special province of the young, the learning community will make education the concern of **lifespan learners.** The lifespan learner will be prepared for continuous social and cultural change, to contribute to the economic vitality of the community, to expand our common cultural heritage through the worthwhile use of leisure time, and to help in strengthening community institutions.

But how is all of this to be accomplished? We must begin by allowing people to establish a new and very different relationship with postsecondary education. Americans now want their courses offered twenty-four hours a day and at convenient locations. They want high quality, but they want the cost to be reasonable. **What today's learners demand is a different kind of education: community-based education.**

For community colleges, community-based education embraces a learner-centered philsophy. First, it places the learning needs of the student above the teaching needs of the institution. Second, the institution determines its missions, goals and objectives through active diaglogue with the community. Third, the community college's programs and services must focus on the knowledge and skills that the learner requires to be an effective, productive member of the community (McGuire, 1988).

The college that is dedicated to community-based education will also take a more proactive approach to addressing community needs. It realizes, for example, that those who are most in need for its services are often the most reluctant to seek them out. This community college will reach out through a wide array of credit and noncredit courses, community services, industry-specific job-training programs, or even aid in forming a small business, as Kentucky's Hazard Community College now does. It will become a catalyst, a convener, and a cooperator, all in the spirit of helping the community become self-reliant and self-sustaining.

Guiding Principles

BUT WHAT PRINCIPLES SHOULD GUIDE THE COMMUNITY COLLEGE AS IT takes up the challenge of building learning communities through lifespan learning? We believe that there are five: (1) citizen empowerment, (2) community renewal, (3) the promotion of broad access, (4) the use of technology, and (5) continuous assessment.

• Empowerment

Few will disagree that a participatory democracy requires an empowered citizenry. Empowerment is not only vital to the achievement of each individual's full potential, but essential to the development of community and the preservation of democracy. But we must go beyond these platitudes. The community college's commitment to empowerment must extend to people of diverse backgrounds, many of whom have gone unserved by traditional forms of education. We must accept that America's minority subcultures have been by-passed by society's institutions, including schools and colleges. We must change our organizations and our practices so they are more open, reflect many cultures, and embrace people from all backgrounds. We must also be proactive in bringing about this change. We must reach out, issue invitations, and initiate personal contacts. We must show that we care about everyone's involvement and experience. We must reaffirm that people of diverse backgrounds matter (DeHart, 1992, p. 27).

But what is the relationship of empowerment to education? The dictionary defines empowerment as "giving power or ability". Those who are empowered possess the competence to work within a social and political system. They are invigorated and inspired to achieve the highest level of performance (Byham, 1988). They take ownership of what they do—whether it is improving themselves or their community. Because empowered people have both information and responsibility, they bring an incredible power for good to the community (Carlzon, 1987). But a prerequisite to empowerment is education! Indeed, it is education's very purpose to empower individuals to live competently and fully within their communities.

• Community Renewal

Communities require continuous renewal. Without renewal, individuals face frustration, disorientation, and dismay. Organizations suffer stagnation, and communities can look forward to their own disintegration. Simply put, communities must become more concerned with renewal if our society is to survive. But renewal does not mean the uncritical reaffirmation of the past. Rather, it signifies finding new solutions appropriate to the world we are entering, a world of diversity, instant communication, and constant change.

Some community colleges have responded to this imperative, providing exemplary programs that showcase the positive outcomes of an institutional commitment to renewal. But even those colleges most concerned with renewal have attended more to the needs of individuals than to those of organizations. Too many in our community colleges continue to act as though the teaching of particular subjects and the awarding of marketable credentials is education's sole objective. While understandable, this view is too narrow for our changing times. A community-building college must concern itself with the renewal of organizations as much as individuals. The community is more than a collection of men and women operating independently of each other. We all act in the context of cultural, social, and political organizations. To truly help the community renew, community colleges must take the lead in the improvement of all its working machinery.

● The Promotion of Access

Already, some colleges promote community development through nontraditional modes of organization: open community colleges, open campuses of multi-unit colleges, and noncampuses. The success of these noncampus colleges should make us all consider Arthur Levine's probing question (1995): "Are we as educators engaged in the learning business or the real estate business?"

Recognizing that successful organizations must be positioned in line with their strategic vision, the organizational pattern we recommend for the prototype learning community is a network of partnerships modeled after Lipnack and Stamps's concept of "TeamNets." This pattern has the potential of empowering individuals as it addresses community problems and the needs of learners through coalitions that network across disciplinary, institutional, community, and even national boundaries (1993, p. 10).

We envision that these local partnerships will be made up of self-reliant community organizations and informed individuals drawn broadly from the community. These coalitions will be the vehicle for creating the learning environment that taps fully into our collective potential. Unbound by tradition, they will pilot new management strategies in the areas of planning, curriculum development, and comprehensive support services. And, by their very nature, they will encourage a community-wide concern for broadly accessible and learner-centered instruction.

● Technology Rich

The knowledge explosion means that individuals will have no difficulty in securing knowledge and information. The challenge is rather to ensure that it is equitably and effectively delivered to all in keeping with the **knowledge utility model**, where each learner can access—anytime, anywhere, through transparent technology—the knowledge he or she needs for empowerment and self-renewal. While we do not recommend that a community deliver all information via technology, educational providers should complement traditional methods with a technology-rich system to ensure cost-effective and equitable delivery.

Already, the technology required by the learning community has been invented or is on the drawing board. What is needed now is a redefinition of classroom parameters. We must come to accept the possibility of virtual classrooms that allow for "real time" interaction between learners and teachers despite constraints of time and space (Lever, 1992, p. 2). Already, tele-conferencing via cable or satellite is breaking down the barriers of space and time. But technology will not end there. Levine (1995) envisions a not-too-distant future in which virtual reality allows students in New York and Japan to enroll in the same course at Miami-Dade Community College and have the sense of sitting in the same classroom. By the turn of the century, Joel Orr predicts (1995), such students will be able to turn to each other in a virtual classroom and share electronically translated comments.

Indeed, prototypes of technology-based learning networks are already in place, and the community colleges that ignore these new providers may soon find their traditional methods rendered obsolete. Already, Mind Extension University (ME/U) is offering college credit via personal computer and/or television (Yasuda, 1995, p.E1). Affiliated with twenty-five universities, ME/U reaches twenty-six million American homes and has created its own accredited college to supplement its programming. It now serves nearly 40,000 enrollees and has recently joined with the Colorado community college system to offer accredited courses over ME/U's cable-TV network.

● Continuous Evaluation

As community-building colleges become more active in their communities, we believe they must continuously reexamine every aspect of their organization and embrace change where it is needed. In effect, the first order of business of the community-building college is improved assessment (Tate, 1995).

Assessment tied to regional accreditation provides the foundation for continuous institutional evaluation. But a community college must move beyond these requirements and develop that broad perspective required to evaluate itself in terms of its new mission. The community college must now consider whether its practices, policies, and methods help the community achieve its goal of promoting lifespan learning and whether its community service strategies result in broad-based renewal. Is there effective communication between the college and the entire community, and not merely community leaders? How well has the college worked toward the vision of a true learning community in the face of increasingly restrictive external controls? To what degree can the college achieve this vision through its partners, rather than solely through its own efforts?

Barriers to the Community-Building Mission

T HE ROAD TO THE LEARNING COMMUNITY WILL NOT BE EASY. WITHIN the academic community itself, there are those who argue that the community college should not embrace this broader mission. Dougherty and other critics of the community-based mission argue that the community college narrow its focus to university-parallel programs (1994). They defend a narrow role on historical grounds, arguing that the two-year college was established to provide lower divisional undergraduate study. They claim that added curricular functions have "distracted" the community college from its "proper" mission at great cost to traditional students and overall institutional effectiveness.

These arguments are simply without basis. Almost from the beginning, the community college has been expanding its mission, driven by a unique calling to extend opportunities for personal and community growth to every American. Established in the early 1900s in response to a local need for a preparatory school for the university, the community college moved quickly after the passage of the Smith-Hughes Act in 1917 to address local employment needs by adding vocational and technical programs. By the 1930s occupational-technical education had become a permanent and major component of its curriculum.

With the passage of the Adult Basic Education Act in 1964 (PL 89-750) and encouraged by such prominent educators as Cyril Houle and B. Lamar Johnson, community colleges expanded their mission further, to offer programs for the lifelong learner through its community services function. A decade later, the AACC formally embraced community-based education by calling on community colleges to adopt programs and services that address the most pressing community needs.

Without question, the present mandate to build communities is a direct continuation of this line of development. It fulfills the promise of the community services function described more than three decades ago by Ervin L. Harlacher (1969, p. 70):

> Through its community dimension, the community college can provide opportunities for raising the cultural level of its citizens, betterment of occupational status, development of community leadership, and an educational climate in which the citizen can develop his potential.

For Harlacher community services was to be far more than a few noncredit classes or the occasional performance by a touring orchestra. Harlacher argued that it institutionalized a distinctive philosophy of education that recognized the college as society's primary means of extending formal and informal education over the length and breadth of the community (Pedersen, 1993). In speeches and publications (1964, 1968, 1969, 1970, 1973) Harlacher rejected any limit on the scope of a program he believed to be essential to community revitalization and renaissance. Community services programs were the means, he argued, by which a community's "standard of life" could be renewed in all its facets.

It was not long before the community services philosophy began to redefine the total curriculum of the community college. As James F. Gollattscheck observed (1989, p. 7):

> ...people in our field have wished for a community college in which community services and continuing education were not a sideline, but the organizing concept of the entire college.... I submit that community colleges are about to become colleges of community service and continuing education.

And this evolutionary process is not over. Our nation and its community colleges are on the verge of a more comprehensive community-building mission, in which they respond to community needs by building learning communities (O'Banion, 1993). A college that embraces this mission will emphasize individual empowerment and community renewal in every program and in all of its services. It will understand that central to its role is the development of new ways to realize the goal of a true learning community, even to the extent of breaking with long-held approaches to education.

We can best understand the tremendous potential of the learning community through examples. One especially promising example is to be found in Battle Creek, Michigan. With support from the W.K. Kellogg Foundation, Kellogg Community College has joined forces with Battle Creek's public schools, library, and museum to define a new ecology of human learning for the community. Using available technology and broad-based institutional collaboration, the Battle Creek prototype has created a more knowledgeable citizenry. Local citizens set goals and learn in a self-directed manner from an expanded lifespan learning agenda. And this is only the first stage in a truly millennial transformation.

But even as learning communities take form around the nation, real challenges must still be overcome. For one thing, we must improve the quantity and quality of information provided key policy makers at the state and federal levels, lay governing bodies, and the media about the learning community and its tremendous potential to renew communities.

At the national level, community college leaders can accomplish this through the community college literature, through involvement of community-building colleges in consortia, and through national community college organizations. At the local level, broad acceptance of the college's community-building mission can grow from the strategic planning process and the town hall meetings described later in this work. We can point out the obvious savings that come from collaboration and the ability of education to empower individuals. And, at a time when politicians are prone to cite "an era of limits" as an excuse for inadequate funding, we should not hesitate to point out the political wisdom of lifespan learning.

Of course, adequate funding is the most formidable barrier to the learning community. Currently, no states and few districts allow tax monies to fund the total array of activities associated with the true learning community. But while much remains to be done to secure public funding for the learning community, committed colleges need not wait on state and local governments. There are alternatives. Businesses, government agencies, media, foundations, professional associations, and individuals all have an interest in promoting innovation.

One option, noted by Albert L. Lorenzo (1995), is the "shadow college." Cost-effective and highly successful, these college units are often fully supported by contracts with employers. Another largely untapped funding source is tuition reimbursement. A recent study found that less than seven percent of eligible employees use this benefit. Tate (1995) has argued that community college should take the lead in convincing employers to shift to tuition prepayment rather than reimbursement, arguing that such a shift could double or triple the participation rate.

Certainly the most obvious funding source for the learning community are federal programs. For example, some community colleges finance assessment services through participation in the Department of Labor's One-Stop Career Center grants, while others have discovered a new source of funding through the "EZ" program. However, we must give a note of caution. The learning community should not build its programs and services solely on federal funds and expect continued or stable support. Federal funding varies greatly from year to year, and federal grants are often meant only as seed money to initiate a program. The best use of federal funds is on an interim basis, to demonstrate the value of the community-building philosophy to lay governing boards and other policy makers, leading to more stable funding.

Another barrier can be found in the assumptions of some community college administrators and faculty. Those staff members who do not believe that education is for everyone, or that it can occur anywhere, or that the goals of learners are more important than predetermined, faculty-set goals can hinder progress. To ensure such commitment, new approaches to faculty and staff recognition and rewards may be required.

One approach that a college could consider would be a two-tier staffing system, with a more traditional tier for existing senior staff and a more flexible tier for new staff. Lorenzo (1995) reported that this is now being done in the area of fringe benefits and that the City Colleges of Chicago have implemented a two-tier work load. Richard Alfred (1995) has described a "market foresight approach" which places existing full-time faculty who are "really gifted" into a separate contractual category, as the staff of what he called an "educational enterprise." These faculty, selected on the basis of their success in empowering students to achieve learning outcomes, respond to RFPs requiring them to use the latest technologies and methods to better serve student needs.

Reflections

THE CREATION OF LEARNING COMMUNITIES WILL REQUIRE BROAD-based, coordinated effort. And while the community college clearly has no monopoly on community leadership, it is the best positioned to bring together diverse community elements to this end (Boone, 1992, p. 9). After all, its tradition of service has given the community confidence in its capacity and commitment to bring about individual empowerment and collective renewal at the grass roots level (Vaughan and Gillett-Karam, 1993). Community colleges are also generally sensitive to community needs and have considerable experience in working with other organizations to address them. And they are open-door institutions, accessible to a diversity of people, and are experienced in offering courses and services at off-campus locations and in adapting emerging technologies to the needs of learners.

However, if the community college is to take the lead in putting forward this new agenda of social regeneration, it must first reinvent itself as a community-building institution that aims to improve all aspects of community life. It must embrace a relationship with the community based on the pooling of competence and resources. It must work to establish the mutually beneficial partnerships that are essential to a coherent, future-oriented community learning system. Seymour Eskow (1988) described this new role as "part of, creator of, the learning web of each community, linking in the ecology of learning, with the other adult agencies concerned with the welfare of the people of the community" (p. 31).

CHAPTER 11

Anticipating the 21st Century

Planning for learning communities cannot occur in isolation, oblivious to the powerful forces reshaping our world. We must not ignore the challenges these changes pose for the community-building college. How grave will be the difficulties, and how exciting the possibilities?

This planning must begin with the recognition that America's communities are threatened by fragmentation and division, triggered by profound demographic change and an emerging global economy. In just four generations, America has gone from a rural to an urban to a suburban nation, as the focus of its economy has shifted from agriculture to manufacturing to service. Modern transportation and communication systems, in particular, threaten to break down local belief systems and cultures under the weight of a valueless cosmopolitanism. Is it any wonder that the security many Americans once felt has given way to a pervasive sense of uncertainty?

If our communities are to endure, their leaders must first understand these changes and what they imply for the task of building learning communities. We must look to changes in technology, lifestyles, demographics, public policy, and the workplace for evidence of what our new world will be like (Lorenzo, 1995). Only then can we hope to prepare our communities for the world they will inhabit decades in the future, and not simply for today.

21st Century Change Drivers

This work has its own vision of the future, and it is a vision that underlies and shapes our call for fundamental change. To better ground the reader in an understanding of our vision, we have grouped our discussion of the most significant trends—what we call **change drivers**—and their implications for the community college under three broad headings: the mosaic society, the information-based economy, and the learning society.

● The Mosaic Society

Once our nation was characterized as a "melting pot" society. This view was first put forth by Hector St. John de Crevecoeur in 1765, and even now describes our collective ideal of social harmony and order (1940). But in the waning years of the 20th century, profound demographic change has remade the American nation (Cetron and Davies, 1989; Toffler, 1990). These trends have combined to dim the luster of de Crevecoeur's ideal. Increasingly, we recognize that America is a mosaic society, made up of many communities, with widely differing needs, but which must still come together if they are to solve our nation's most pressing problems.

ETHNIC DIVERSITY

The transition from the melting pot to the mosaic society began in the 1980s, during a time of large-scale immigration, when almost nine million people came to this nation. By 1995, foreign-born U.S. residents had reached the highest pro-

FIGURE 1

PERCENTAGE DISTRIBUTION U.S. POPULATION BY RACE: 1980–2050

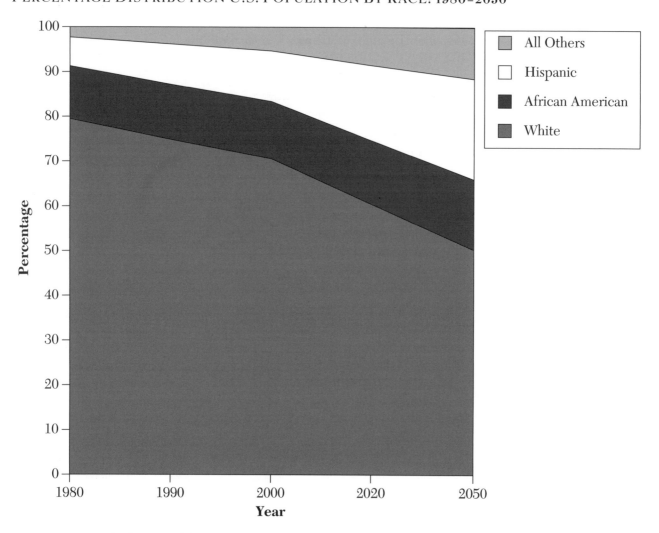

Source: Statistical Abstract of the United States, 1994; U.S. Department of Commerce, Bureau of Census

portion of the nation's total population since World War II—8.7 percent. More-over, in contrast to earlier waves of immigrants, those who arrived were over-whelmingly Hispanic and Asian. During the 1980s America's Asian population more than doubled, while its Hispanic population grew more than 60 percent.

Nor will these trends reverse themselves. As a percentage of the whole, America's white population will decrease significantly, while African Americans will decrease slightly. Hispanics, Asians, and Native Americans will, however, grow rapidly. By 2000, nearly one in three Americans will be a member of a minority group, and California, our most populous state, will have become the nation's first minority-majority state. By 2030, if Cetron and Davies (1989) are correct, minorities will constitute a majority of all Americans (Figure 1).

Many Americans have welcomed these changes and have called for a new social order based on pluralistic principles. They recognize that individuals from

FIGURE 2

MEDIAN AGE (U.S.): 1980–2050

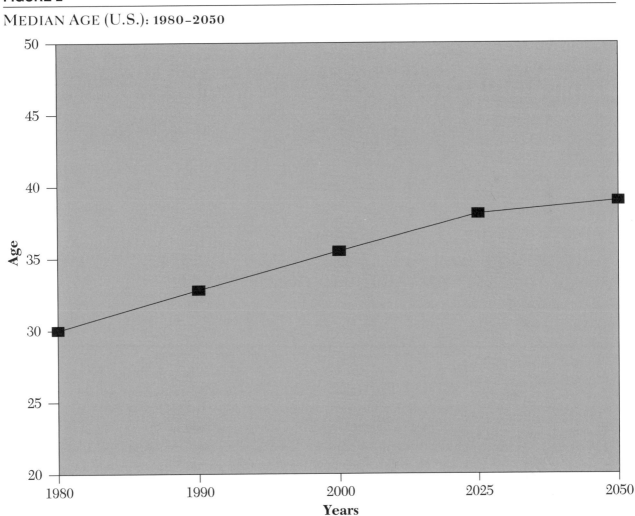

Source: Statistical Abstract of the United States, 1994; U.S. Department of Commerce, Bureau of Census

diverse cultures can come together, converse, and learn from each other while retaining their own distinctiveness and value, just as they recognize that the nation's survival will depend on its ability to capitalize on this diversity. We must not see our nation as divided, but more as a tapestry, made rich by its colors and variety, and as only made stronger by lifelong learning.

THE MATURING OF AMERICA

The population of the United States is graying. Daily, the number of Americans over 65 grows by 1,600. By 2000 the United States will be a nation of adults, as "Baby Boomers" continue to age while birthrates lag. Even though the total U.S. population will increase 24 percent between 1980 and 2010, those over the age of 25 will increase by 32 percent. The median age, now close to 33, will reach 41 by 2030. By 2050 it is likely that 25 percent of Americans will be 65 or older, outnumbering teenagers more than two to one (Figure 2).

Community colleges have already seen the consequences of this trend in the age distribution of their students. As early as 1980, the mean age of community college students was 27. By 1986, the mean had increased to 29, and by 1991, it surpassed 31 (Cohen, 1996, p. 41). Now well more than half of all older students enrolled in higher education are attending a community college. But the signficance of this demographic trend will not be limited to the ages of students in college classrooms. It will be felt broadly through our economy and culture, leading to a fundamental redefinition of the "natural" life pattern. The traditional "linear life plan" will be replaced by a **cyclic life plan** (Dychtwald and Flower, 1989). Where once education was solely for youth, work for the middle aged, and leisure for the elderly, education will now play a central role in the lives of all adults, regardless of age. This is already happening, as colleges increasingly recruit older Americans, but the real pressure for change will come with the broad realization among Americans that the mind does not grow old, only obsolete, and that lifespan learning can keep it vital and young.

NONTRADITIONAL FAMILIES

The mosaic society will be organized around an increasing number of non-traditional families. Single-person households, single-parent families, and same-sex households could well outnumber traditional, nuclear families early in the next century. Already, one in four households is made up of a single person, while one in four children is born out of wedlock. This trend will forever change our society and the way education responds to individual and community needs.

Of particular importance to educators should be the growth in the number of single-parent families, for these families face extraordinary challenges in our changing world. Even now, these families are disproportionately impoverished, comprising 41 percent of all poverty-level families (Coates, 1990). And in the future they face the prospect of a lessened federal commitment to the "social safety net" and no real guarantee of state support to assist them in gaining the skills needed to secure stable, well-paying employment.

EMERGING ROLE OF WOMEN

Women will assume a dominant role in the American labor force of the 21st century, constituting almost 60 per cent of all workers by 2000 (Cetron, Rocha, and Luckens, 1988). By this point, nearly eight of ten adult women will be working, compared with just 64 percent in 1989. Working, even for mothers with young children, will be an accepted part of American life. Unfortunately, the traditional role of women as wives and mothers has not changed nearly as rapidly as their role in the labor force. The result has been tremendous tension for those who must balance these roles (Cross, 1981).

Given their tradition of accessibility to women, community colleges should expect that new demands will be placed on them, in particular, to empower women to compete for jobs and status without sacrificing the well-being of their families. We should begin planning now to organize educational delivery in ways that allow for more flexible hours, childcare, eldercare, and new alliances with business that can lower the cost of and stress of learning for women.

TABLE 1

DISTRIBUTION OF U.S. EMPLOYMENT BY MAJOR CATEGORY

1983-2005

	1983	1994	2005
Executive, Managerial	9.4	10.2	10.4
Professional	12.3	13.6	15.5
Technicians	3.3	3.5	3.7
Managerial/High Skill	**25.0**	**27.3**	**29.6**
Marketing/Sales	10.3	11.0	11.4
Clerical/Support	18.4	18.2	16.7
Service	15.2	15.9	17.2
All Services	**43.9**	**45.1**	**45.3**
Agricultural and Related	3.6	3.0	2.5
Crafts 12.40	11.1	10.3	
Operators/Laborers	15.0	13.5	12.4
Other Skilled	**31.0**	**27.6**	**25.2**

Source: Statistical Abstract of the United States, 1994
U.S. Department of Commerce, Bureau of the Census

• The Information-Based Economy

The second of our three change drivers is America's shift from an industrial to an information-based society. The emerging information-based economy will be marked by a dramatic increase in the availability and complexity of information and by equally dramatic increases in individual freedom. The democratization of information will free us all to try the new and untested. It will allow us to organize our lives in unprecedented ways.

KNOWLEDGE-DEPENDENT SOCIETY

Employment data highlight the extent to which America's economy has already become information-based. In 1950 only 17 percent of the jobs in America involved the processing of information, by 1980 more than half of American workers were either creating or distributing information (Cetron, Rocha, and Luckins, 1980). By 2000, some estimate that 80 percent of workers will be employed in the information industry (Table 1).

But the change is not simply in the distribution of work, but in its very nature. Some experts even predict the demise of the traditional job as the way American's organize their work. Calling the job "a social artifact," William Bridges (1994) has predicted that businesses will increasingly rely on a contingent workforce, able to reshape itself as circumstance dictates. The growing use of part-time and temporary workers is, for Bridges, an early indication of this fundamental change in the nature of work.

Further evidence of this change can be found in the extent that the computer has broken down the work-home barrier. As Lewis (1992) reported, by 1991 a majority of home offices used computers and more than 39 million people did all or part of their paid work at home. We should expect the number of home workers will grow as telecommuting proves increasingly attractive in those urban areas, such as the Los Angeles basin, where transportation expenses and pollution-control regulations impose greater costs on those employers and workers who continue to separate home and work.

In the new world of contingent workers, the importance and relevance of education can only increase, because knowledge will be the basis of job security and wealth. "New knowledge," Earl Joseph observed, "leads to new ways to increase the quality of life and standard of living, and produces jobs that didn't—couldn't—exist before" (1984, p. 133). And unlike traditional forms of wealth, knowledge will not be bound to any one place. The resistance of some American leaders notwithstanding, traditional notions of nationalistic self-interest will continue to yield to international trade cooperation as the universalization of knowledge compels developing and developed countries alike to accept liberalized trade.

• The Learning Society

The third of America's "change drivers" is the emergence of the learning society. Americans are no longer complacent about the need to focus national attention and energy on education. We see evidence of this new energy in efforts to eradicate illiteracy, to expand training and retraining opportunities, and to reform the schooling system itself (Naisbitt and Aburdene, 1990). These forces will bring about a revitalized educational system whose implications have obvious and profound significance for any community-based strategic planning.

LITERACY GAP

Literacy has become a pervasive concern of our society. A shockingly large number of our citizens cannot read simple statements or conduct transactions necessary to daily life. The statistics are both staggering and depressing (Best and Eberhard, 1990; Davidson and Koppenhaver, 1988): 27 million American adults are illiterate, another 47 million are considered functionally illiterate, and as many as 25 million more need to update their skills and knowledge. Nor does the future hold much promise for quick change. Even now, 30 percent of all high school students drop out before graduation, while the rate is a staggering 51 percent for Hispanic and African American students, and two of five high school graduates are functionally illiterate.

Yet literacy is the very thread weaving together the learning society; its importance cannot be overstated. Nor should we define functional literacy narrowly as simply the ability to read, write, and compute. Ever-advancing technology requires us to expand the definition to include, at a minimum, computer, civic, and informational literacies. Even the entry-level competencies required of most workers include the ability to solve problems independently and to respond with flexibility to new situations. While some state legislatures and even some college leaders have called for colleges to surrender any concern for literacy development to the public schools, the pervasiveness of the problem demands that literacy remain a major focus of community college concern and activity.

TRAINING AND RETRAINING

There will be an increasing need for job training and retraining in the 21st century. Our job is no longer simply to educate young adults entering the nation's workforce, if this workforce is to meet the challenge of global competition (Twigg and Doucette, 1992). As the workforce ages, future service-sector growth will focus more on productivity gains through technological advances and more effective employee-training programs.

It will be in the interest of everyone to be fully involved in continuous education. Every current job will be in jeopardy by 2000. Workers will be continually displaced and only find reentry to the world of work if they possess needed skills. According to experts, we can expect to be "re-careered" throughout our lives as one job slowly evolves into the next. Dychtwald and Flower (1989) cited a Rand study that predicts that by 2020, workers will each need an average of thirteen retrainings during their lifetimes.

Fortunately, community colleges have already taken a strong leadership role in meeting retraining needs. As Doucette and Roueche noted, "community colleges have become one of the principal providers of training and retraining for a workforce being buffeted by changing demands" (1991, p. 2). We expect that the growing national emphasis on training needs and retraining will encourage a broad range of agencies to increase their involvement in education by forming partnerships with community colleges and businesses, bringing closer the ideal of collaboration that must be at the heart of the new learning community.

A NEW LEADERSHIP STYLE

True reform of education will demand a new brand of leadership. The successful leader of the 21st century will be less a commander than a coach, who will find culturally-appropriate ways to inspire individuals to embrace common values and purposes. Meeting the challenge to prepare community college leaders who do not acquire power through authority, but by inspiring commitment, will be the special challege of 21st century graduate schools.

Reflections

THE THREE CHANGE DRIVERS DISCUSSED IN THIS CHAPTER REPRESENT major challenges. Although we cannot know what the future holds, it would be irresponsible for community leaders to assume that the great changes are now past us, and that the nation and the world are entering a period of stability. But if community colleges are to shape the direction of change to the benefit of their communities, they must enter into a new relationship with these communities. As we will discuss more fully in Chapter III, community colleges must establish a relationship based on the concept of the community as campus and client.

The Community as Campus and Client

We define the term "community" not only as a region to be served,
but also as a climate to be created
          Commission on the Future of Community Colleges, 1988.

As we have argued above, the challenges of the next century will be met through revitalized communities—learning communities—with the community college as their very nerve center. For communities to effectively play this role, they must come to see and accept **community as campus and client**.

Fortunately, the concept of community as campus and client is not new to the community college. Several writers have envisioned such an intimate relationship, foreseeing its central importance to the emergence of true learning communities. Among the first to advocate that colleges look beyond their campus boundaries were Ervin L. Harlacher and Gundar Myran.

In 1969, Harlacher observed:

> The philosophy that the community college campus encompasses the length and breadth of the college district, and that the total population of the district is its student body, makes it possible for the community college, in a massive and untraditional way, to broaden the base for higher education (p. 3–4).

Shortly thereafter, Myran (1974, p. 4) envisioned a time when community colleges would be the leading force in bringing together all education providers in a collective effort to build the learning community:

> The community-based college will, in this new climate, view itself not as the exclusive educational center of the community, but rather the agency which weaves the fabric of post-high school education—wherever it happens in the community and in whatever form—together.

Others have since called on community colleges to broaden their involvement in the full life of the community. Max Tadlock (1978) suggested that colleges expand the community-based model to include the entire community as the student body. For Tadlock, no college could be truly community-based until it stepped through its own open doors and into the community. In the same spirit, Edmund Gleazer (1980, p. 16) described what he felt should be the new mission of community colleges: "to encourage and facilitate lifelong learning, with community as process and product."

Defining the Community

BUT WHAT, ONE MIGHT REASONABLY ASK, IS THE "COMMUNITY" THAT community colleges should serve? If it is more than merely a geographic location, what are its characteristics and parameters? Without question, we agree with Gardner (1991) and his rejection of the traditional notion of community as a homogeneous grouping based in part on exclusionary practices. Neither can we accept a parochial notion of community, as simply consisting of people who live in close proximity.

Our definition of community begins with the dual recognition that while the quality of life greatly depends on our ability to effect a sense of community, changes in technology, the nature of the economy, and communications have broken down the traditional association of community with place. The bonds of community have been dissolving for many years. Gardner (1991, p. 8) described this wholesale deterioration and its consequences. Men and women torn lose from a context of community and shared values, he explained,

> often experience…a loss of meaning, a sense of powerlessness. They lose the conviction that they can influence the events of their lives for the community (noncommunity) in which they live. And one striking consequence is a diminution of individual responsibility and commitment.

But there is also hope, as Americans awaken to the need to restore community. We can see this reawakening in the Communitarian Movement's emphasis on the vital importance of shared family and community values to the preservation of individual rights and a vital democracy (Communitarian Network, 1993, p. 1). We can see it when the Futures Commission (AACC, 1988, p. 7) pronounces that

> the building of community, in its broadest and best sense, encompasses a concern for the whole, for integration and collaboration, for openness and integrity, for inclusiveness and self-renewal.

To all of this, we would add that the essence of community is empowerment. The community college confers upon its members an identity, a sense of belonging, and a measure of security. Its absence destroys the anchors of the individual, and so threatens each of us with the disintegration of society.

A Viable Community Model

THIS SAID, WHAT ARE THE PRINCIPAL ELEMENTS OF THE REVITALIZED community toward which community colleges should all work, and how can they best realize this ideal? First, we must approach our task with certain assumptions. One, it must be a given that community-building begins at home. For a community college, this means that it should strive to model the means and desire for effecting a sense of community. As Lawrence W. Tyree (1990, p. 4) wrote, "if the college first becomes a community internally, it will then reach out more effectively to the larger community…truly serving it."

Second, a community college should adopt the broadest possible understanding of "community." From the perspective of the Futures Commission, a community college service area does not constitute simply a convenient geographical or political arrangement, but a region of shared interests, needs and values. And, as Etzioni reminds us (1993), the community college is essential to community well-being, for communities, like families, depend on core institutions. If you rob communities of their vital institutions, they deteriorate. But if you build up institutions, the entire community grows and prospers.

Further, the college must recognize that there is no longer one best learning site. Learning is valuable and legitimate wherever it takes place. Indeed, the effectiveness of sites can vary by time and mode of instruction (Nickse, 1981, p. 221). We do not suggest that traditional uses of a campus are invalid, but that people must be free to learn in every imaginable setting as their needs and interests dictate. Some will prefer the traditional campus, its degrees, and its large lecture halls. However, far more learners find an ivy-walled campus inconvenient and uninviting.

Finally, the community-building college must commit itself to three fundamental changes. First, it must understand the importance of viewing its community in terms of core organizations. It must also recognize the need to working collaboratively with these organizations in partnership to deliver needed educational services. And it must be willing to transform its curriculum following the principles of community-based programming.

• Change 1: Focusing on the Community and Its Organizations

There are, of course, many characteristics of a community which affect and ultimately determine its total quality. Some constitute its infrastructure, such as parks, buildings, and roads. Others shape its environment, such as its abundance (or lack) of natural resources. But the most important component of any community is its people, especially when joined together in groups devoted to shared interests, for only they can experience the reciprocal concern required for community-building.

An individual and his or her community each depends upon the well-being of the other. Only people can strengthen communities, but they depend no less on communities for their strength. When communities weaken, individuals lose their support systems, and eventually the individual cannot help the community, nor can the community empower the individual. Moreover, while one person may have a great impact on a community, groups must mobilize for important and lasting change to occur.

Constituencies are a convenient way of grouping organizations, and provide a framework for community colleges to focus their efforts and energies toward fundamental change. As we will show, constituencies can be generally divided among four basic types of organizations: associations, charitable organizations, government agencies, and businesses. Whatever their specific form, all four types have three aspects in common. First, their members share a purpose and act in concert in the context of that purpose, thus becoming more than the sum of the individual members. Second, each organization has unstated as well as stated purposes. In fact, it is not uncommon for unstated purposes to exercise greater influence on the organization than any formal statement. And third, each organization has a distinctive mode of operation. This may be as formal as an elaborate policy manual, or as informal as a loosely followed set of operating procedures.

Associations are composed of individuals who band together to advance a specific or limited purpose. Membership is generally voluntary, although some larger association may retain some professional and support staff. Of all community organizations, associations are the most numerous and the most varied. Forms of association include special-interest groups, often with a relatively narrow focus; ethnic associations, concerned with the promotion and preservation of their shared culture and heritage; associations dedicated to the interests and causes of women; and neighborhood and civic improvement groups. Associations of this latter type are especially helpful allies, since they share a common purpose with the community-building college: the betterment of the community.

The second type of community organization is the **charitable institution**, created to address some specific public good: education, health, or charity. These organizations are more formally structured than associations, often holding a charter from a state legislature, local government or, as in the case of the Red Cross, from Congress. They are more likely to own or lease buildings and other facilities and maintain a paid staff. The public may be involved through memberships, for which a fee can be charged or a contribution expected, and charities may receive direct payments for services. Charitable institutions may be either tax-supported or nonprofit.

City, county, state, and federal government agencies constitute the third organizational type. Agencies include such entities as courts, commissions, law enforcement and welfare units, parks and recreation departments, to name but a few. Agencies are tax-supported but may charge fees.

Government agencies frequently need training for employees and are generally very willing to plan joint programs. For community colleges, law enforcement has been the most fruitful area of cooperation to date, because of increased federal funds. Agencies are also charged with providing services to constituents (as through JTPA programs) and frequently subcontract some of these services to community colleges. The image of the college as an effective service provider within the community will be enhanced by cooperation with governmental agencies.

While the benefits of cooperating with the fourth organizational type, **businesses**, are generally self-evident, they are too important to omit. While businesses are profit-motivated organizations, this does not need to be an obstacle to cooperation. Because businesses need employee training, they are generally willing to pay for it. They also value long-term associations with educational institutions and often support these institutions through gifts of funds, facilities, and expertise. Recent interest in partnerships with businesses, promoted heavily at the national level by AACC, has caused this area of community collaboration to become the most active of all.

Of course, in giving this much emphasis to groups as vehicles for community renewal, we should not forget that some individuals will be included in several groups, while many others will not be associated with any group at all. Moreover, it is not always easy to weigh the relative significance of any one constituency. Especially with associations, the more organized and vocal a constituency is, the more likely it is to be recognized, yet any prominence acquired in this fashion reveals nothing significant about a constituency's size, the seriousness of its needs, or its capacity to serve as a community resource and partner for the community college.

● Change 2: Building a Learning Community Through Partnerships

In an era of ever-greater fiscal constraint, no one organization, including the traditional community college, can bear sole repsonsibility for the creation of the learning community. But the community-building college can bring together other organizations, as partners, to make learning accessible through technology-rich delivery systems subject to rigorous ongoing evaluation.

A community college will find that many, but not all, associations noted above are appropriate for joint endeavors, for they are already deeply involved in providing adult learning. These associations consider education integral to their missions. Like community colleges, they seek to make people more knowledgeable, more aware of needs and concerns, or more skillful in solving problems, and many prefer what they offer. Two-thirds of all adults now involved in formal learning programs take courses sponsored by employers, labor unions, government agencies, community organizations, private entrepreneurs, and others. Businesses are reported to spend more money on employee education and training than the total amount spent by the postsecondary sector. And increasingly, for-profit businesses, from Internet providers to book publishers, see providing educational opportunity to adults as a source of growth and profit.

But each of these associations typically carries on these efforts independently, leaving a community's learners with the daunting task of sorting through any number of educational providers for solutions to their problems. In the interest of the learner, we expect that the community-building college will recognize what is being done by these other providers and take the lead in using partnerships to create a seamless system of community-based educational providers that will form the foundation of the learning community. If the community college does not model and lead this educational transformation, Bernard R. Gifford quipped, "it is difficult to envision who will" (1991, p. 2).

Those who might question this coordinating role fail to understand that community colleges, with the broadest operational base, are ideally positioned to bring focus to a community's educational efforts and to thereby reverse systemic community decline. Moreover, colleges—especially those in more rural communities—have the expertise and standing to assist other providers with complex program planning and development. But most importantly, they have a well-deserved reputation for selfless community service, making them the institutions best able to bring to the table a wide array of organizations and interest-groups.

The critics of the coordinating role also ignore the very real benefits of partnerships. As pointed out by Doucette and Roueche (1991), the willingness of community colleges to collaborate with business in meeting its training needs has already earned colleges increasing support, while enabling businesses to keep the American workforce competitive. Collaboration also allows for the conservation of resources, enabling all organizations to respond better to community needs. Learners will benefit directly from cooperative arrangements, as the confusing array of programs that now confront them would be integrated and made more accessible. And communication between the college and the community will be improved. As Paul Elsner (1995) has noted, American communities are in constant transition, and community-based organizations are the best informed about emerging needs. Through collaboration, a community college can gain access to this vital information.

But most importantly, collaboration can enhance the credibility of the college in the community's eyes, as it demonstrates the college's genuine interest in working with community organizations. We must not forget that a community college's interaction with external groups determines how it is perceived (Gollattscheck, 1983, p. 21).

MODES OF PARTNERSHIP AND COLLABORATION

Collaboration encompasses a wide range of strategies. For purposes of clarity, we identify four basic modes of collaboration: advisory relationships, direct assistance, joint ventures, and mergers.

The **advisory relationship** is the most common form of college-community partnership. The use of advisory committees by colleges is already widespread, but the college-building college should expect its own staff to be increasingly used as advisors to community organizations as these organizations come to better understand the reciprocal nature of partnerships.

Through **direct assistance**, an educational provider contributes services or other resources in support of a specific educational initiative. Direct assistance may entail a college providing a program or service for an organization or vice versa. These arrangements may be of any length and are often more formal than advisory relationships. For this reason, it is generally best that such partnerships be based on a contract, especially where they involve any substantial resource commitment.

Direct assistance arrangements are most common where a community organization lacks the means or expertise to undertake a critical, immediate task. In this way, Catawba Valley Technical College in North Carolina provides direct assistance to the state's furniture industry. The college maintains a laboratory that is, in fact, a small-scale furniture factory. Through the laboratory, the college offers a series of courses under contract specifically tailored to the needs of North Carolina's furniture industry.

Joint ventures are higher-level collaborations, and their relative formality generally requires a contract to detail roles and obligations. An ideal joint venture pools the unique strengths of each partner, where each knows something about the other and, above all, where there is mutual respect.

Joint ventures hold tremendous potential for community development. Through such a venture, Laredo Junior College, the Texas Department of Agriculture, Hebrew University in Israel, and Texas A & I University created a 135-acre demonstration farm at the college, to develop fourteen alternative crops for the arid regions of the Rio Grande Valley and west Texas. The venture helped to create 25,000 new jobs and $6.1 billion of new business for the Texas economy.

As the learning community materializes, we can expect that **formal mergers** between colleges and organizations will become increasingly common. In a merger, the partners recognize that they have a common interest in meeting a critical need, and that they can best meet this need by creating a separate corporate entity.

The Arcadia Commons in Kalamazoo, Michigan, is a $100 million, three-block testament to the benefits of mergers. Kalamazoo Valley Community College (KVCC) instigated a community effort to build a business-education park in downtown Kalamazoo. With First of America Bank Corporation, the Upjohn Company, and the Kalamazoo Public Museum, KVCC formed Downtown Kalamazoo, Inc. Working with the city government, the new corporation secured a $1 million federal grant to further the project and obtained tax-increment financing. Later, Upjohn spent $18 million to renovate the downtown Kalamazoo Center, an aging convention-hotel-retail complex, into a five-star Radisson Plaza Hotel.

But a word of admonition! Before a community college enters into any collaborative arrangment, it must decide if it is willing to share aspects of administration that have been its sole prerogative. A community college should first ask itself:

- Is it willing to share responsibility for the planning and operation of a partnership, recognizing the staff commitment partnerships require and the necessity for shared management?
- Is it willing to share the credit for successes? Is it willing to sacrifice some immediate publicity for long-term good will?

• Change 3: Establishing a Community-Based Curriculum

Only through its curriculum can an educational provider achieve its mission. Where mission and strategic vision chart an institution's path, curriculum is the vehicle by which this mission is achieved. It follows, then, that all issues concerning curriculum must be addressed in the context of prior decisions about mission.

In adopting a mission as a community-building institution, a community college must continuously ask itself two questions: (1) what kind of curriculum, with or without degree or certificate requirements, will provide what the people of our communities want and need to know, and (2) how can such a curriculum be developed?

The curriculum of the community-building college must be grounded in partnerships. While the college will continue to address those needs for which it has the resources and expertise, it must also serve as a catalyst to bring together other organizations to resolve those issues requiring resources beyond its immediate control (Vaughan and Gillett-Karam, 1993). It must turn a community's educational efforts into a unified whole, emphasizing the "connecting links" among all educational programs (Gollattscheck, 1981, p. 61).

Of course, this does not mean that a community-based curriculum will ignore "the hierarchies of knowledge" that prevail in our cosmopolitan culture, even where they may not be valued within a community or, in rare instances, they may conflict with fundamental community beliefs. This curriculum will recognize that individual empowerment and community renewal come about through a process of dialectic, in which community beliefs and values are set against those of the larger culture (Pedersen, 1993, p. 4).

Further, the community-based curriculum will not be a warmed-over version of a traditional curriculum. It recognizes that not everyone wants or needs credits, degrees, and credentials, and it therefore offers alternatives. It recognizes that even those with degrees need lifelong learning. What it strives for is collaboration in the production of programs that teach those competencies needed to address community problems and individual needs.

Perhaps the most comprehensive model for the community-based curriculum has been developed at North Carolina State University. As described by North Carolina State's Edgar J. Boone (1992, p. 2), community-based programming is a cooperative process, in which a community college becomes the "leader and catalyst" in drawing an area's organizations and agencies together to overcome common challenges.

Boone's model assumes that community colleges never work alone in achieving their social purposes. The model defines a process by which community colleges become the moving force in promoting greater collaboration. This model also demands that a community college reexamine its mission in keeping with its community-building role and that it reposition itself as required (Vaughan and Gillett-Karam, 1993). As developed through the ACCLAIM project, this model has led Charles County Community College, Maryland, to confront head-on the issue of rapid transition from a predominately rural service area to a suburban one, just as it has led Southside Virginia Community College, Virginia, to collaborate with other service providers in addressing the special needs of single women with dependent children to acquire job skills and related competencies.

Programs and Services of the Learning Community

With the learning community as its goal, what programs and services does the community-building college encourage? We can assume that its programs will anticipate and reflect demographic, societal, and technological changes, be based upon carefully documented needs of the community and be accessible to all who need them. These programs will also employ performance-oriented methods and focus on developing those competencies needed by learners to solve community problems and meet their individual needs. They will provide traditional credits and degrees only where such credentials are clearly necessary.

Already, many community colleges are working closely with their communities in taking the first programmatic steps toward building a curriculum for the new learning community. Some are addressing the needs of the emerging mosaic society. Others are preparing for the new information-based economy, while still others are forging the partnership links essential to the learning community itself. For models, we can point to:

- Red Rocks Community College, Colorado, which uses the Johnson County public elementary schools to provide GED and English as a Second Language classes. The college provides special scholarships to defray tuition and on-site child care expenses.
- Illinois Central College, whose Self-Employment Training (SET) program assists low-income and unemployed people in starting their own businesses. Its three components include a 78-hour, nontraditional classroom segment that culminates in preparation of a viable business plan; a communitywide "Partnership of Opportunity" project in which public and private entities contribute resources toward long-term training and economic development of minority-owned businesses; and a five-year consulting service to assist in the reduction of small-business failures.
- Lake Michigan College's Project Together, which teams the college with the Berrien County Social Services Department to promote self-sufficiency among mothers on public assistance through a structured program of counseling, job training and other self-management services. Program assistants, who were once themselves on public assistance, work with participants to address total family needs by identifying family and individual strengths, rather than focusing only on the participant.
- Chemeketa Community College, Oregon, which has collaborated closely with Cascade Steel Rolling Mills to ensure worker mastery of computerized steelmaking. The college custom-designs training and delivers it on-site on a schedule that accommodates the company's three-shift production schedule.
- Women in High Innovative Technology Studies (WHITS), a nontraditional vocational program for rural women, which addresses disparities in orienting Appalachian women to nontraditional careers in industry. The program, offered by Southwest Virginia Community College, provides an introduction to computer-aided drafting, electronics, and bio-medical technology, while building math and English skills.
- The Elder Institute of Daytona Beach Community College, Florida, which offers leisure-time courses in dance, art, and music, and seminars on retirement planning. Leadership training is the centerpiece of the institute's program, which recognizes older Americans as a significant political constituency. The college absorbed the cost of opening the insti-

tute and plans to complement its commitment with both public and private funding.

Reflections

COMMUNITY-BASED EDUCATION, IF FULLY IMPLEMENTED AS WE HAVE described it, represents a radical departure from conventional thinking about postsecondary education. Community-based education is committed to the proposition that human renewal—the empowering of every person—is education's primary and overriding purpose, and it places the learning needs of the student above the teaching needs of the educational provider. "This may sound very commonplace at first," as Gollattscheck suggested in 1977, "but when one considers it in the light of all of the history of postsecondary education, it is quite revolutionary" (p. 2).

Community-based education also recognizes the interdependence of a community. In the face of rapid change, a community's very future will depend upon the vitality and flexibility of its partnerships, and it must be the community college that takes the lead in providing coordination and direction to the orchestration of these partnerships. Many community colleges have made progress in building the foundation of the learning community through partnerships, and such efforts must be recognized, supported, and extended.

PART II

Giving Life to the Community Strategic Vision

UNDERLYING THE ARGUMENT OF THIS WORK IS OUR CONVICTION THAT **vision** is our lifeline to the future. Through vision, "we can create our own future, but we have to see clearly what changes are occurring and think clearly what our purposes are so we may remain loyal to our philosophy" (Hankin, 1992, p. 40). When a community lacks a compelling vision, its development will be haphazard, constantly swayed by the latest fad or most recent advice. But, as Peter Senge (1990, p. 354) puts it, when people throughout the community share a larger sense of purpose, they are united in a common destiny. "They have a sense of community and identity not achievable in any other way." When change is managed and directed by those with vision, we can look to the future with hope.

But where does the process of community building begin? In the following three chapters we will outline a process by which a college and its community can define a common vision of the future and translate that vision into needed programs and services. Central to this process is the community college. When reconstituted as a **community-building college**, the community college can be the catalyzing agent for this vision and this process. Beyond the community college, our process also requires broad community participation, extensive environmental scanning, and strong leadership. This participation will be assured through the leadership of a Joint Steering Committee and various specialized task forces, as well as through the extensive use of town hall meetings. As basic as America itself, the town hall meeting is the one decision-making format that can bring together diverse community representatives to reach consensus on strategies for carrying our communities forward to realize the great potential of learning communities.

CHAPTER IV

Initiating the Planning Process

OUR TIMES REQUIRE A NEW PLANNING APPROACH, ONE THAT IS FLEXIble and dynamic. Traditional planning techniques merely project present and past trends into the future, and so are weak in identifying environmental changes and assessing their institutional impact (Morrison and Mecca, 1990). These techniques wrongly assume that a community's environment is static and composed of relatively few variables.

Today, strategic planning must be *proactive, long range, and community-based*. It must address multiple issues, avoid operational hierarchies, and promote public consensus on community issues (Kemp, 1990). And most importantly, strategic planning must rigorously assess people's lifespan learning needs. What we will call **community strategic planning** strives to strengthen the community college's relationship to its larger community by continuously refining the purposes and processes of both.

McClenney, LeCroy, and LeCroy (1991) have observed that effective strategic planning depends upon several preconditions: leadership commitment, broad participation, a clear focus, the integration of outcomes with the mainstream of institutional decision-making, simplicity, and an action orientation. We would add that because of its broad participation, community strategic planning must be effectively structured. By following a process of four distinct phases—**preplanning, direction-setting, diagnosis, and implementation**—communities that undertake the complex task of strategic planning can be assured that the task will achieve its goals in an orderly and timely manner.

Preplanning

AS ONE MIGHT EXPECT, THE PREPLANNING PHASE CONSISTS OF SUCH tasks as identifying task leaders, orienting participants, and specifying timelines and responsibilities for the overall planning process. We have summarized these responsibilities under three general headings: establishing a Joint Steering Committee, indentifying relevant planning resources, and the establishment of workable timelines.

● Establishing a Joint Steering Committee

The planning process begins with the designation of a Joint Steering Committee to give overall guidance and leadership to the strategic planning effort. This committee is essential to the process. It should be representative, with membership drawn equally from college and community leaders, and large enough to ensure that each task force it establishes is chaired by a member of the committee. Those selected for membership should also be knowledgeable of organizational dynamics, familiar with the challenges facing the community, and committed to college-community collaboration.

The success of the Steering Committee will depend on the visible support of the college president and key community leaders. To reinforce this support, committee co-chairs should be named, with one each coming from the college and the community. No less indicative of support for the Steering Committee are the staff and research resources it is allocated. Among these resources should be a planning coordinator. The coordinator can either be an outside consultant (which would guarantee that a skilled strategic planner is involved and that the process poses no additional burden on an already busy manager) or an internal facilitator trained by an outside consultant.

At the outset of the process, the coordinator should orient the committee and other interested parties to the project, including the major planning tasks and the general principles of strategic planning. This is frequently done at an all-day workshop. Depending upon the sophistication of those involved, the coordinator may also want to include an explanation of research and study techniques.

● Identifying Relevant Planning Resources

Also at this early stage, the coordinator should obtain copies of existing college and community research, planning studies, and reports. To facilitate their use by the Steering Committee and its task forces, the coordinator should compile this information in a loose-leaf data book for each participant in the planning process.

● Establish Workable Timelines

Critical to the success of the planning process is early agreement on an overall project design. Components of this design include project timelines, procedures, and respective responsibilities. This task is frequently completed by the coordinator for adoption by the Steering Committee.

In preparing a timeline, the coordinator should expect the planning process to require an intensive nine- to twelve-month commitment. In addition to the ongoing tasks of the committee and its task forces, the process can include at least four town hall meetings to ensure "immediate reaction and interaction among those from whom support is needed" (McClenney, LeCroy, and LeCroy, 1991, p. 49).

The coordinator should also plan for at least monthly meetings of the Steering Committee to ensure open communication, easy interaction, and prompt feedback. As questions of turf and conflicting values arise, it can also arbitrate disputes (McClenney, LeCroy, and LeCroy, 1991). Task forces can be expected to meet even more frequently, as the needs of the process dictate.

Direction-Setting

DIRECTION-SETTING IS THE SECOND PHASE OF THE STRATEGIC PLAN-ning process. It is concerned with the broadest type of strategic thinking and seeks to provide a general framework for the diagnostic and implementation phases of the planning process. Experience tells us that community initiatives are most productive where consensus on the big picture is reached first, before any consideration of specifics. Experience also tells us that consensus is most likely to be achieved through a town hall meeting.

To assist with direction-setting, the Steering Committee should appoint its first task force: the Strategic Vision Task Force. The specific responsibilities of this task force, which should have eight to twelve members, include the organization of the first town hall meeting to assist in the formulation of strategic goals to guide the planning process. Based on our experience, we strongly recommend that the task force utilize the charrette process as the basis for the operation of the first town hall meeting.

• The Charrette: An Overview

A charrette is a group-based strategy for achieving broad consensus on difficult or complex issues. It is a proven method for bringing the best out of a town hall meeting's participants. Gollattscheck and Richburg (1981) have outlined the elements of a successful charrette. These include:

A **commitment** on the part of the charrette's sponsors to implement any reasonable solutions that result from the process. In turn, participants commit themselves to the time required by the process and to the proposition that solutions are best reached through groups working within strict time limits.

Open-mindedness on the part of participants. Participants must agree to put aside preconceived solutions and fixed attitudes. Sponsors must also have an open mind about process outcomes and must communicate this openness to all participants.

Diversity of participants and resource people. Not only must those involved in a charrette reflect their communities, they should also represent a broad range of backgrounds, philosophies, and experiences.

Follow-through on the charrette process. Responsiveness by a charrette's sponsors is critical to success. The invigorating sense of accomplishment participants gain from a charrette will be reinforced if they receive timely copies of the summary report of their meeting and other tangible evidence that their efforts are valued.

● Organizing the Charrette

Any group process enjoys success in direct proportion to the quality of the planning that preceeds it. Therefore, the Strategic Vision Task Force should address each of the following steps prior to the first town hall meetings (Gollattscheck and Richburg, 1981; Puyear, 1991):

SELECTION OF THE CHARRETTE LEADER

The charrette's basic simplicity can lead to the misconception that the process does not require an experienced leader. This is not the case. A charrette leader must possess a number of qualities. He or she must be thoroughly knowledgeable about charrette management—from necessary physical and logistical arrangements to the working of group dynamics. The charrette leader must be someone whose expertise is respected by the participants, since he or she must at times be arbitrary or directive to keep the process on track. At the same time, the leader must also be responsive, having alternative strategies ready to move the group to consensus. As a practical matter, it is often best to select a leader from outside the community.

ARRANGEMENT OF APPROPRIATE FACILITIES

Because of its intense atmosphere (the pressure of time is not only inevitable, but essential to success) a charrette requires facilities that allow participants to immerse themselves in the process. This virtually mandates a retreat or hotel setting, where participants can be kept free of outside distractions. The meeting room should be large enough (preferably ballroom size) to seat each team at a table comfortably and still provide room for flip charts, overhead projectors, and other resources.

SELECTION OF PARTICIPANTS

Because of the visionary tasks of the first town hall meeting, the Strategic Vision Task Force should select participants who represent a broad spectrum of perspectives and interests, the major political and/or geographic subdivisions of the community, and key college constituencies. We recommend that 80 to 100 persons be invited, since the charrette process does not work well when there are not enough participants to field at least four teams of eight to ten persons. However, to attempt to work with more than ten teams, or with teams with more than ten members, can be unwieldy.

PARTICIPANT ORIENTATION

Well in advance of the charrette, participants should be informed in writing of what they can expect. They should be informed of starting and ending times, the mission and purpose of the meeting, how the process works, what they are expected to contribute, and what is to be their product. It is especially important to impress upon each participant that there is limited time, little opportunity to get additional information, and a requirement to reach consensus. Feelings can run high. Unless there is a genuine desire for consensus, the process can fall into disarray and participants can withdraw from the discourse.

SETTING THE MISSION

Establishing a specific mission for the meeting is another key to its success. At this stage in the planning process, the mission of the first town hall meeting would be to articulate a vision for the college as a community-building institution in the form of broad strategic goals.

SELECTION OF TEAM LEADERS

Once an agenda is set, the task force should select team facilitators and synthesizers from among the meeting's participants. The facilitators' responsibilities include chairing the charrette teams, keeping the teams on schedule, and cultivating creativity and encouraging participation. Unlike the facilitators, the synthesizers play a less proactive role. In addition to serving as team recorders, synthesizers play a critical role during the process in bringing teams to closure on ideas or recommendations.

● Operation of the Charrette

The operation of a charrette is actually quite simple. The event begins with the assembled participants receiving a brief orientation to the process from the leader. It is essential for the leader to emphasize three key rules at this point: no ideas will be attributed to a particular participant, all participants must have an equal voice, and the leader has the only clock and timetable.

Following their orientation, the participants break into teams. The teams meet for a specified amount of time on an assigned task and utilize brainstorming or other techniques to respond to their task. The entire group then meets to hear reports from each team (often presented with visual aids) which are then juried by a panel of peers to facilitate group consensus. If consensus is not reached by the total group, the team recommendations may be referred to a small task force or editorial committee for additional work, followed by a second presentation to the entire group. The recommendations of each team, including the final consensus, are recorded on flip charts and ultimately incorporated into a written transcript of the meeting. This process is followed until the agenda is completed and consensus has been achieved on all tasks.

In our specific instance, the charrette leader might guide teams in brainstorming a list of the ten most important needs facing their community. In developing their lists, teams might describe the major challenges the commuity faces, its resources, and its shared values. This latter task is very important, since many of the values that have shaped our society are taken for granted.

Addressing community values directly would ensure that the charrette's strategic goals reflect a vision "firmly rooted in humane values that are currently lacking in too many of our societal institutions" (AACC, 1988, p. 49).

A second task could be for participants to select from this list a number of strategic goals and to prioritize these goals in terms of those that would most benefit from educational solutions. After there is agreement on this prioritized list of goals, participants might then discuss how these goals would impact on various community constituencies. Through this process of small-group-large-group jurying, deleting, combining, and rewording, the participants can produce a manageable number of critical problems amenable to educational solutions, which would then form the basis of the strategic goals needed to guide the diagnostic and implementation phases of the strategic planning process.

After the conclusion of the charrette, the Strategic Vision Task Froce should submit its strategic goals to the Steering Committee for review and option. Adoption of these goals would conclude the first part of the direction-setting phase of the planning process.

CHAPTER V

Diagnosis

DIAGNOSIS IS THAT PHASE IN THE PLANNING PROCESS WHEN THE Steering Committee, guided by the first town hall meeting's strategic goals, gathers the data and information required for its strategic plan. The key tasks of this phase include futuring and the scanning of the college and its community.

Futuring

IN THE FACE OF PROFOUND CHANGE, ONLY STRATEGIC FUTURING CAN enable a community and its college to fulfill their potential. Through futuring we can "suggest things that might happen in the future, so that people can decide what they want to make happen" (World Future Society, 1991, p. 1). To carry out this phase of the planning process, we recommend that the Steering Committee appoint a Futures Task Force of eight to twelve members drawn from the community and the college.

The first responsibility of the Futures Task Force would be to identify key trends in the life of the community using environmental scanning techniques. Scanning is a form of radar, which systematically surveys the world for evidence of the new and the unexpected, and which allows us to sort through data and other evidence, highlighting those trends with the greatest potential for impact.

Depending on local circumstances, planners can use a variety of approaches in environmental scanning, from brainstorming with a panel of experts to formal studies employing sophisticated analyses. The specific technique for futuring we recommend is a modified version of the ED QUEST planning model. The ED QUEST process requires two full-day meetings of the Futures Task Force (usually separated by about a month). To assist the task force, we recommend that college staff complete a simple environmental scan prior to the first meeting of the task force.

• The Task Force's First Meeting

At its initial meeting, the Futures Task Force would use the environmental scan prepared by staff to examine the external environment and to identify major trends in the life of the community. This task is more complex than it might at first appear. A **trend** (as, for example, a predicted general decline in state appropriations to higher education) may be suggested by one or more specific events (a recision by a governor, lower tax receipts, or the like). But not all events imply a trend (Lapin, 1992). The task force must be extremely careful not to be distracted by any single event, however immediately significant, when it is attempting to identify trends, for the event may well be an isolated occurrence.

The task force would then select those trends it would want to further analyse. One method it might use is a Delphi survey. In the Delphi process, each participant would take a list of future trends identified by the task force and assign a numeric value to each based on a judgment of its probability of high impact. These estimates are then collected and displayed to the group, which either concurs on the relative value of each item or holds another Delphi round. This process of probability estimation is especially important, for it enables the task force to focus its attention not simply on significant trends, but on those trends with the greatest probability of occurrence (Nanus, 1989).

Once the Delphi process has been completed, the task force should focus its attention on those near-term **critical events** that are to be the most likely outcomes of these trends. One technique of identifying these events is the futures wheel. The futures wheel can is especially helpful in augmenting simple brainstorming in generating the "discrete, confirmable occurrences" known as critical events (Morrison and Mecca, 1990).

To construct a futures wheel, the task force begins by selecting one probable trend (e.g., "women will play a more significant role in the labor force") to serve as the hub. The group must then agree unanimously on the three to six critical events that they expect to result from this trend. These events constitute the first level of the wheel. The task force then completes the second level of the wheel by coming to agreement on several impacts that will follow from each of the critical events included in the wheel's first level (Phi Delta Kappa, 1984). While a third and even a fourth level of the wheel may be completed in the same manner, we would recommend that the task force limit itself to two levels in order to leave sufficient time for building consensus and charting future directions.

Once identified, these critical events must be prioritized, so as to narrow the group's focus to a manageable ten or fifteen events. In the process of prioritization, the task force can also describe their key events in increasingly precise language. Where, for example, the initial statement of a critical event might have been written "there will be an expansion in the number of educational providers," it would become "nonpublic educational providers become more than fifty percent of the community education industry by 2000."

The task force would then conclude its first meeting by evaluating the interaction among its critical events. One technique to measure this interaction is the **cross-impact matrix**, described by Nanus in helpful detail (1989). From our experience, this is an excellent tool for weighing the likely effect of critical events on the community. As described by Nanus (1989, p. 206), the use of a cross-impact matrix can assist a small group such as the task force to create a "mental model of how the world is expected to work in the future, and how these critical developments relate to the...[community and college's] business."

• The Task Force's Second Meeting

The second meeting of the Futures Task Force should take place about a month later. During the interval, a summary of the first session should be prepared by the planning coordinator and circulated to members. This allows the second session to open immediately with a review of the summary report, a discussion of any subsequent insights by task force members, and the reporting of any new advice received from experts or community leaders.

The princpal responsibility of the task force during this session is the development of written **scenarios.** These scenarios capture alternative futures and allow the task force to identify and prioritize strategic issues that emerge from these scenarios. The task force should synthesize the trends and critical events identified in its first session into three written scenarios: best case, worse case, and most likely case. Each scenario (which essentially answers the question, "What would happen if such and such occurred?") should be internally consistent, plausible, and sufficiently detailed to be useful in the next stage of the strategic planning process. Through the writing of scenarios, task force members must analyze, group, and compare information and identify any internal inconsistencies.

Finally, through brainstorming and the Delphi process, the task force would abstract **strategic issues** from the scenarios. Strategic issues arise out of trends and events and suggest the potential for conflict or controversy. This step of the futuring process is especially critical, because the issues identified here will have a significant impact on the overall strategic plan.

• Finalizing the Process

Following the second task force meeting, a town hall meeting should be held to review and affirm the futuring process. Major tasks of this meeting include the assessment of the three scenarios and the review of the strategic issues. The town hall meeting should conclude its work by recommending a single scenario for further consideration as part of the strategic planning effort.

When the futuring process is finished, the result is not only a written scenario envisioning the community's future, but detailed knowledge about the interconnectedness of trends, critical events, and emerging strategic issues as they affect the lives of the community and the college. At this point, a high degree of consensus will frequently emerge among participants as to the best direction to be pursued by the community and the college as they move into the future.

Internal Scan

DURING THE DIAGNOSTIC PHASE, THE STEERING COMMITTEE SHOULD also name a College Assessment Task Force to assess the college's relationship to the community. This task force would focus on those aspects of the college's role and mission that may require change because of external trends identified through the futuring process. By carefully weighing the college's circumstance and capacities, the task force will not only inform the strategic planning process but help to improve college operations generally (Morrison and Mecca, 1990).

The Steering Committee must know the internal strengths and weaknesses of the college to develop a comprehensive picture of its present condition and to assess the feasibility of any long-range proposals that come out of the planning process. For this reason, the task force will analyze the college's internal condition by studying management audits, program evaluations, and student course evaluations; by assessing the needs and perceptions of faculty, staff, and students; and by reviewing current and potential resources. The college's planning or institutional research offices should be a principal source of this information. Other sources can include program reviews, self-study reports, and advisory committee recommendations (McClenney, LeCroy, and LeCroy, 1991, p. 23).

The External Scan

I N ASSESSING THE COMMUNITY WE SEEK TO DETERMINE ITS TOTAL STATE of health. The community-building college must sense changing needs so that it can effectively address immediate problems and anticipate future problems. It must have a continuous flow of information from the community. Even more importantly, however, to do this it must be able to translate great amounts of unorganized information into concrete problems that the community can solve based on its new understanding of its strengths and resources and its potential for self-improvement.

To assist in carrying out the responsibility of an external scan, the Steering Committee should appoint a Community Assessment Task Force. In scanning the community, this task force will complete a number of activities, including determining the scope of the scan and the identification, collection and analysis of critical data.

● Scope of the External Scan

With the goal of fashioning a true learning community in mind, the Community Assessment Task Force should begin its work by considering quantitative and qualitative questions to be posed of the community. Among its quantitative questions, the task force might consider identifying the demographic composition, major constituencies and organizations, and principal strengths and weaknesses of the community. Among its qualitative questions, the task force might explore the community's commitment to change, the effectiveness of organizations in carrying out their respective functions, and the unmet needs of individuals. In forming its questions, the task force should be sensitive to danger that it will focus too intensely on the future, and so avoid critical issues of the present. It is easy to talk about future employment growth, but that should not blind us to the reality of current, systemic unemployment. The task force should pay as much attention to the current state of the community as to its hopes for the future.

Successful community assessment will also require extensive and meaningful community involvement in the development of the research design. We suggest that the task force schedule two intensive planning sessions, drawing participants broadly from the community, and consider at least the following questions:

- From whom do we want to hear?
- What do we want to know and why do we want to know it?
- How can we best elicit information from a particular constituency?

• Sources of Data

Certainly it makes sense for the task force to begin by reviewing available information, evaluating its accuracy and usefulness, and identifying gaps in existing data bases. It can then address those gaps incrementally by seeking new information sources, by building on existing research efforts, or by designing entirely new research initiatives. Community assessment is a continuous process, and its initiation need not wait until all possible research has been completed.

The most easily accessible source of general information on communities is the US Census Bureau, which regularly collects a broad range of demographic, social, and economic data. Many are familiar with the bureau's decennial studies, but it also issues a steady stream of specialized reports on a wide range of topics. Many other governmental and private agencies regularly report useful data. Most state finance departments publish reports on schools and other agencies. State and regional planning boards collect and compile data reports. Associations also gather data, and many conduct surveys to apply for public or private grants.

An invaluable source of information on the community are state employment agencies. In many states this office regularly compiles employment information by major industry group, including unemployment rates and worker demographics. Because creation of strategic goals and implementation strategies requires a detailed grasp of the roles of all local education and training providers, the external scan should include an inventory of these providers, their funding mechanisms and the extent of their coordination. It should also assess the needs of various education clienteles (e. g., high school seniors and transitional workers).

The task force should also consider locally produced research. Many communities have research or planning councils, which coordinate surveys and other forms of data collection and ensure the general availability of these studies. And as colleges have become more proficient in marketing analysis and prediction, they have also gathered a wealth of data about their local environments.

Neither should faculty and students be ignored as a source of information and as participants in its collection. In many respects, community college students are a mirror of the larger community, especially of those under age 35, and so could be studied directly as part of the community-building exercise. Moreover, as part of their individual professional development, faculty and staff might conduct research on various aspects of the community, and their results incorporated directly into the work of the task force.

● Gathering Data

In approaching available data sources, the task force should understand that no one research method will work well for all community constituencies and organizations. In the case of employers, for example, any survey should be conducted face-to-face or by means of a telephone interview. Although many researchers contend that an employer survey is not a valid means of determining real occupational needs, it often validates data produced by other research and affords the "employer community" active involvement in the process of needs assessment. Similarly, staff members of agencies and associations should be surveyed independently of their organizations' leadership, for these staff members will play a critical role in interpreting the strategic vision for their constituencies.

● Analyzing the Data

The task force should conclude its data analysis by recommending general planning assumptions about the state of the community's overall health. These assumptions are essential to the formulation of a community strategic plan, for they represent the plan's basic parameters. They should consist of integrated statements, offering a comprehensive profile of the community and a projection of its future in keeping with the scenarios adopted by the second town hall meeting.

These planning assumptions should enable the Steering Committee to pinpoint remedies for current and future problems. By revealing the capabilities, mutual interests, and established relationships among community constituencies, these assumptions open the way to greater collaboration. They will almost certainly reveal a great many educational providers within the community, just as they will show that there is a lack of coordination and leadership essential to community strategic planning.

Direction-Setting (Stage 2) Revising the Institutional Mission

IT WILL BE NATURAL FOR SOME TO SEE THE GOAL OF A COMMUNITY strategic plan in terms of a discrete document or report. However, focusing on finished documents as the most important outcome of this process implies finality and inflexibility, both qualities inconsistent with the true learning community. The community strategic plan is better described as a flexible set of proposed directions—what we initially termed "strategic goals"—grounded in shared community values. The direction-setting phase of the planning process (which actually overlaps the diagnostic phase) concludes with the translation of these goals into a new mission for the community college as a community-building institution, with the identification of critical success factors and an assessment of strategic options.

To assist in this effort, the Steering Committee has its strategic vision, confirmed by the first and second town hall meetings, as well as the results from its futuring initiative and from its external and internal scans. It is now positioned to formulate a new mission for the community college that will include the identification of critical success factors and strategic options. Because of the complexity of this phase of the planning process, the Steering Committee may wish to appoint a Mission Revision Task Force, constituted in essentially the same manner as its other task forces. The specific role of the Mission Revision Task Force will be to reasses the college's mission, to identify critical success factors and to develop strategic options.

● Mission Revision

Possibly using brainstorming techniques, or reaching out to the community through the use of focus groups, the Mission Revision Task Force must first reasses its college's mission. Guiding this effort should be the following questions:
- What should be the college's specific function and scope as a community-building institution?
- What is the community-building college expected to deliver, and to whom?
- What difference should such a college make in the lives of community learners?
- How much responsibility does the community college have for maintaining the community's social fabric, securing its economic well-being, preserving its history and culture, and strengthening its values and beliefs (Lorenzo, 1995)?

● Success Factors

As its second task, the Mission Review Task Force will identify benchmarks for evaluating the college's performance in achieving the **critical success factors** that will directly reflect achievement of its mission as a community-building college. Critical success factors are key institutional measures in such areas as effectiveness, efficiency, cost, and competitive advantage that make the difference between organizational success or failure (Rockart, 1979). They consist of those factors that most people would agree are significant to the institution's well-being.

Midlands Technical College (SC), as part of its strategic revitalization effort, identified six critical factors. These included comprehensive, quality programs with quantifiable outcomes, the retention of satisfied students, economic development and community involvement, effective resource management, and dynamic organizational involvement. We might suggest other success factors as well: (1) overall commitment of college leadership to the community-building philosophy, (2) accessibility of the college to the people of the community, (3) comprehensiveness of programs and services offered to meet community strategic goals, (4) satisfaction and retention of learners, (5) effectiveness of resource management, and (6) cost-effectiveness of program delivery.

Most likely using brainstorming techniques, the Mission Revision Task Force would develop its list of critical success factors. Then, possibly through a Delphi process, the members can identify and rank between five and ten of these factors as the most significant. For example, the task force might select such factors as completion rates, service utilization, and expenditures per student contact hour (Hudgins, 1990).

● Strategic Options

As the final direction-setting task, the Mission Revision Task Force will finalize community strategic options. Among these options might be the greater use of collaboration and joint ventures to achieve the decentralization of education throughout the community. In two to three hours of brainstorming, the task force should be able to identify more than a hundred options. It would spend the remainder of its time assessing its options in terms of their relative feasibility, risks and rewards, resource requirements, and relevance to the goal of building a learning community.

The Steering Committee will receive the final direction-setting recommendations of the Mission Revision Task Force and submit these recommendations to a town hall meeting for final approval through the charrette process. The new statement of mission, and the description of strategic options, will form the basis for the implementation phase of the community strategic planning process.

CHAPTER VI

Implementation

I NCLUDED AMONG THE IMPLEMENTATION TASKS FACING THE JOINT STEER-
ing Committee will be the design of a community-based curriculum, the
selection of an operational model and adopting a plan of continuous process
evaluation. At this critical juncture in the process, the committee must translate
the community's new, shared strategic vision into concrete programs and services and new partnership strategies. It must also establish a framework for the
continuous evaluation of these new initiatives.

Curriculum Implementation

I N KEEPING WITH OUR EARLIER CALL FOR COMMUNITY-BASED EDUCATION,
it is our conviction that fundamental curriculum change should follow
the revision of a community college's mission in keeping with the principles of a community-building college. It is also our argument that these curriculum changes should follow from decisions concerning an institution's
mission and purpose, and that they should not be the exclusive concern of
faculty and college administrators.

From our perspective, overall responsibility for these curricular revisions
should fall under the Joint Steering Committee, which may find the charrette
process helpful in initiating curriculum planning and development. Participants in a town hall meeting could be given the task of specifying a community-based curriculum to address critical community needs, taking into
account all of a community's available resources, and then classifying these
curricular initiatives in keeping with previously adopted goals. Once the committee receives these curricular specifications, it can then begin the process
of laying out the competencies of the community-based programs appropriate
for each curricular initiative. To assist it in this task, we would recommend
that the steering committee appoint a Curriculum Planning Task Force, drawing its members widely from community-based educational providers and
consumers.

In structuring its work, the Curriculum Planning Task Force may find these
questions (based on O'Banion, 1993) useful:
- What is the role of the community-building college's curriculum in
  responding to difficult social issues?
- How will educational providers fund a more responsive curriculum?
- Is the community college's faculty prepared to take on new roles?

• How should the college evaluate its new curriculum and the faculty members who teach it?

Additionally, the task force should consider carefully the major characteristics of a teaching/learning model appropriate for a future-oriented learning community:

• A climate of inclusiveness that permeates the entire community.
• Acknowledgement that learning takes place over the entire lifespan.
• Recognition that the most important skill for survival in the information age is learning how to learn.

More specifically, the task force should strive for a community-wide system of competency-based education leading to demonstrated mastery of the basic and life skills necessary for the individual to function proficiently in society. Such a system would provide to all, at times and places convenient to them, the kinds of skills, knowledge, and other abilities that are likely to be required of the learner at some later time, in a later course, or on the job. And, no less importantly, this system would require the learner to demonstrate mastery of competencies as an integral part of the teaching/learning process.

The challenge facing the task force in devising such a performance-oriented teaching/learning model appropriate to the needs of its community are substantial. Postsecondary education has yet to systematically devise programs and services that ensure that the kind of skills, attitudes, and knowledge essential to life in our complex society are determined in advance, that the learning process is individualized, and that learning for mastery is achieved. While millions of adults are currently enrolled in educational programs and services there is no systematic means of matching learning to problems and needs, no uniform standard measures for competencies needed and the competencies learned.

Ultimately, the work of the Curriculum Planning Task Force needs to be approved by the Joint Steering Committee at a town hall meeting, in conjunction with the Action Plan recommendations described below.

Implementing Partnerships

A S A FIRST STEP IN DEVELOPING THE PARTNERSHIPS THAT WILL BE required by the learning community, the Steering Committee will need to appoint a broadly representative Operations Task Force. The Steering Committee should set as the task force's first objective the assessment of the community's potential for developing partnership arrangements, educational delivery systems, and organizational patterns appropriate to the learning community. The task force needs to consider which, if any, community organizations have the resources and commitment to contribute to effective partnerships, and what degree of formality these relationships should take.

In its review, the task force should consider:

• The organizations' objectives and whether these objectives are consistent with their commitment of resources.

- The effectiveness of organizations in meeting their objectives, particularly with respect to their use of both internal and external channels of communication to link organizational leaders and their constituents.
- The organizations' physical and human resources and whether these organizations have resources they are willing to commit to joint ventures.

Subsequently, the task force should identify the educational delivery systems most appropriate for the learning community. The Operations Task Force should consider community demographics, based on the findings of the community assessment described earlier, to ensure that any recommended delivery system promotes the ideal of the knowledge utility model. The task force should consider every possible medium, from distance learning and correspondence study to apprenticeships and classroom instruction, with particular attention to factors of cost-effectiveness.

The task force's third objective would be to determine the most appropriate organizational model for the local learning community. The Operations Task Force should give serious consideration to a network-type structure, since this model offers the best prospect of addressing community problems effectively within the constraints of available physical and human resources.

As with the other task forces, the Operations Task Force will need to present its overall recommendations to the Steering Committee. Based on the findings of the Operations Task Force, the Steering Committee can develop and approve a clear, concise statement to guide organizations and educational providers in forming cooperative ventures. This statement might provide guidance on the following points:

- The selection, compensation and supervision of staff.
- The source and allocation of funding.
- Program management and governance.
- The range of programs and services to be provided, and to whom.
- Criteria for project evaluation.
- Conditions for project termination, including the disposition of any jointly-held property.

Given the potential impact of the work of the Operations Task Force on all community organizations, it is recommended that its recommendations be presented by the Steering Committee to a town hall meeting for review and adoption.

Action Plan

A CRITICAL IMPLEMENTATION TASK OF THE JOINT STEERING COMMITtee is development of a five-year action plan. The purpose of the action plan is to make things happen, to point the way for carrying out the strategic decisions adopted in the direction-setting and diagnosis phases of the planning process. To assist in this task, the Steering Committee can name an Action Plan Task Force to develop the specific strategies that will form the core of the five-year action plan. These strategies will form the basis of the first draft of the community strategic plan as well as provide a framework for annual operational plans.

The Action Plan Task Force should address tasks and assignments, assumptions and guidelines, and measurement of progress toward realization of the learning community. It should address such questions as: Who will lead the new learning community and what type of organizational structure will govern the new system? What additional programs and services will be required over the next five years? How would these new programs be staffed, housed and funded? Can costs be controlled without sacrificing quality, and how will this quality be ensured?

The task force should first formulate à list of specific and measurable objectives for each community strategic goal, much as teachers set goals for their students. These objectives must be sufficiently detailed to allow for the assignment of tasks and allocation of resources. These objectives should therefore indicate the specific organizations responsible for conducting goal-related activities and their measurable outcomes.

Next, the Action Plan Task Force will address **strategy**, determining the most appropriate course of action given available resources. The task force should select strategies that will position the community to respond effectively to an increasingly fluid environment. These strategic recommendations should not only designate the desired action, but also the specific college or community constituencies that should assume responsibility for the action, and they should be reported to the steering committee in the form of an Action Plan.

Lastly, the task force will establish budget priorities for the next fiscal year for whatever strategic plan elements fall within the college's responsibility. Priority setting is easy to talk about but difficult to do, requiring both will and skill. But clear priorities are the key to successful implementation of strategic plans and linking of plans to budgets (McClenney, LeCroy, and LeCroy, 1991, 2–3). These critical links between strategic and operational planning commit educational providers, including the community college, to allocate the resources needed to build the learning community. While organizations may express their commitment to this ideal in many ways, they demonstrate this commitment best with decisions, actions, and resource allocations consistent with defined strategic priorities.

These budget priorites are highly focused statements based on specific, measurable objectives developed as part of the five-year action plan and refined as we described above. Representing key priorities for the coming year, they delineate incremental steps toward full achievement of the community strategic goals. They should be limited in number—seven to ten—and supported by an explicit commitment to allocate available resources toward their accomplishment. The task force may wish to use such futures processes as brainstorming and the Delphi technique since they are especially effective in helping groups to set priorities. Their resultant deliberations should be reported to the Steering Committee as an Operational Plan.

This is the final stage in the planning process. Once the Steering Committee reviews and endorses the five-year Action Plan and annual Operational Plan, the Community Strategic Plan is ready for final review and approval at a town hall meeting. The final town hall meeting should focus on clear and concise presentation of the strategic planning documents, preferably by the Steering Committee co-chairs, with emphasis on the Action Plan, which effectively serves as a final executive summary.

Following a concluding town hall meeting, the Steering Committee and staff will finalize the Community Strategic Plan and obtain necessary endorsements from appropriate community and college officials and bodies. It then will disseminate the plan widely. Finally, to ensure that the Community Strategic Plan is successfully implemented, planners should incorporate elements of the Action Plan's priorities into the management objectives of the community college's executive leaders and managers.

Evaluation

BECAUSE OF THE COMMUNITY'S EVER-CHANGING CHALLENGES AND opportunities, the Community Strategic Plan must continuously evolve. To provide for a dynamic plan, the Joint Steering Committee should initiate an annual review process and incorporate any recommended changes in this plan that comes out of the annual operational plans. This provides an opportunity for the committee not only to review the process's overall effectiveness, but to update community strategic goals and to assess the new community-based programs and services and delivery systems. In formulating its review process, the committee may find useful the following questions adapted from the work of Roger Yarrington (1975):

- In what ways do you see the college's programs and services as community-based and performance-oriented?
- How does the college evaluate responses to identified community problems and needs? How are community members involved in this evaluation?
- How accurate are the evaluations?
- How accurately are they reported to the community?
- How well do people in the community understand the reports?
- How are community reactions invited? How well are they received?
- How does the college act on its findings? How does it correct deficiencies? How does it set (and reorder) priorities?
- How well do community members understand the college's goals and programs?
- How do community members form their own informal estimates of the college? How does the college attempt to "read" such informal estimates by persons in the community?
- What could the college do to obtain a better evaluation of its responses to community problems and needs?

Conclusion

IN THE FOREGOING CHAPTERS WE HAVE ARTICULATED A VISION FOR THE 21st century that can position community colleges to respond to the major forces of change. We have also defined a different kind of education for a different kind of student and explained how it might be delivered throughout the community to empower our citizens and renew our communities. In short, we have suggested that America's community colleges provide the leadership for building and rebuilding our communities as true learning communities.

This mission will require an intimate knowledge of the community—of the role each of its members plays in creating and maintaining good community health—and a willingness to allow each element to become involved in the process of renewal. Our communities must develop this knowledge if they are to prosper in a complex, rapidly changing world. Toward this end, community colleges must forge community-wide partnerships, committed to pooling scarce resources and built upon principles of open communication and shared strategic vision.

A college whose goal is to become a community-building college must link with its community to catalyze learning by creating a desire for empowerment and renewal; to assist in identifying all potential clientele by removing physical and psychological barriers to access; to become a facilitator, a referral point, an information center, and a neutral consulting resource through collaboration; to provide a vehicle for community self-education through cost-effective programs based on community strategic goals and an accurate assessment of community capabilities; and to evaluate its own effectiveness.

In this work we have proposed a blueprint for building learning communities by integrating theory and practice. As they carry into their future the imprint of the past and the exigencies of the present, America's communities and their colleges will be constantly buffeted by emerging political trends, major demographic shifts, evolving urban patterns, rapid technological changes, and new economic factors. Only through a structured process of reality-based strategic planning, that is used to guide and assess institutional practice, can our communities rise to the challenges before them.

References

Alfred, R. (1995, April). *Beyond the Horizon: Transforming Community Colleges to Compete for the Future*. Paper presented at the annual convention of the American Association of Community Colleges, Minneapolis, MN.

American Association of Community Colleges. (1985). *Building Communities: A Vision for a New Century*. A Report of the Commission on the Future of Community Colleges. Washington, D.C.

Bell, T.H. (1991). Technology in education in the nineties. *Leadership Abstracts, 4* (7), 1–2.

Best, F., and Eberhard, R. (1990, May–June). Education for the 'era of the adult'. *The Futurist, 24* (3), 23–28.

Boone, E.J. (1992, December). *Community-Based Programming: An Opportunity and Imperative for the Community College*. Raleigh, NC: The Department of Adult and Community College Education, North Carolina State University.

Botkin, J.W., et al. (1979). *No limits to learning*. New York: Pergamon Press.

Bourgeois, L.J. (1980). Strategy and environment: a conceptual integration. *Academy of Management Review, 5*, 25–39.

Boyer, E.L. (1988). An introduction to the Futures Commission's Report. In *AACC. Building Communities: A Vision for a New Century. The American Seminar V Teleconference Workbook*. Washington, D.C.: AACC.

Bridges, W. (1994). The end of the job. *Fortune*, September 19, 62–74.

Byham, W.C. with Cox, J.Z. (1988). *The lightning of empowerment*. New York: Harmony Books.

Carlzon, J. (1987). *Moments of truth: new strategies for today's customer-driven economy*. New York: Harper & Row.

Cetron, M.J., and Davies, O. (1989). *American renaissance: our life at the turn of the 21st century*. New York: St. Martins Press.

Cetron, M., Rocha, W., and Luckens, R. (1988). Long term trends affecting the United States. *The Futurist, 22*(4), 29–40.

Coates, J.F. (1990). Population and education: how demographic trends will shape the U.S. *The Futurist, 24*(6), 10–14.

Cohen, A.M. and Brawer, F.B. (1996). *The American community college* (3rd ed.). San Francisco: Jossey-Bass.

Communitarian network. (1993, August). Washington, D.C.: Communitarian Network.

Cross, K.P. (1981). *Adults as learners*. San Francisco: Jossey-Bass.

Davidson, J., and Koppenhaver, D. (1989). *Adolescent literacy: what works and why?* New York: Harper and Row.

De Crevecoeur, St. John (1940). *Letters from an American farmer, 1782*. Reprinted in L.B. Wright and H.T. Swedenberg (Eds.), in *The American tradition*. New York: Appleton-Century-Crofts.

DeHart, A.R. (1992). Creating our future. *Community College Journal*, 63 (1), 24–27.

Dougherty, K. J. (1994). *The contradictory college*. Albany: State University of New York Press.

Dychtwald, K., and Flower, J. (1989). *Age wave: the challenges and opportunities of an aging America*. Los Angeles: Jeremy P. Tarcher.

Elsner, P. (1995). *Turning the century: creating the transformational learning community*. Paper presented the annual convention of the AACC, Minneapolis, MN.

Eskow, S. (1988). Toward telecommunity college: from open admission to open learning. In E.L. Harlacher (Ed.), *Cutting edge technologies in community colleges*. Washington, D.C.: AACC.

Etzioni, A. (1993). *Leading the community*. Paper presented at the annual convention of the AACC, Portland, Oregon.

Gardner, J.W. (1991). *Building community*. New York: Independent Sector.

Gifford, B.R. (1991). Delivering the promises of technology today. *Leadership Abstracts*, 4 (1), 1–2.

Gleazer, E.J., Jr. (1980). *The community college: values, vision, and vitality*. Washington, D.C.: AACC.

Gollattscheck, J.F. (1977). Community-based education: a new direction for community colleges. *Community Education Bulletin*, October, 1–4.

Gollattscheck, J.F. (1981). Strengthening continuing education in community colleges. In *New Directions for Continuing Education*, 9. San Francisco: Jossey-Bass, 1981.

Gollattscheck, J.F. (1983). Strategic elements of external relationships. In G.A. Myran (Ed), *Strategic management in the community college*. New Directions for Community Colleges, 44. San Francisco: Jossey-Bass.

Gollattscheck, J.F. (1989). Will success destroy community services? or what do you do with the revolutionaries after you've won the revolution? *Community Services Catalyst*, 18 (3), 6–9.

Gollattscheck, J.F., and Richburg, J.R. (1981). The charrette as a group decision-making process for community-based institutions. *Community College Catalyst, 11* (1), 22–25.

Hackney, S. (1995). The American pluralism and identity. Paper presented at the annual convention of the AACC, Minneapolis, MN.

Hankin, J.N. Moving your institution into the 21st century. *Community College Journal, 62* (4), 36–40.

Harlacher, E.L. (1964). California's community renaissance. *Junior College Journal, 34* (8) 14–18.

Harlacher, E.L. (1968). New directions in community services: what's past is prologue. *Junior College Journal, 38*(6), 12–17.

Harlacher, E.L. (1969). *The community dimension of the community college*. Englewood Cliffs, NJ: Prentice-Hall.

Harlacher, E.L. (1970). Community service in the community: a new dimensions in adult education. In M.S. Knowles (Ed.), *Handbook of adult education in the USA*. Washington, D.C.: Adult Education Association of the U.S.A.

Harlacher, E.L. (1971). The community renewal college. *Community Education Journal, 1* (2), 8–13..

Harlacher, E.L. (1973). The community renewal college. *Community Services Catalyst, 4* (1), 5–9.

Harlacher, E.L. (1982). Community general education. In B.L. Johnson (Ed), *New directions for community colleges: general education in two-year colleges*. San Francisco, CA: Jossey-Bass.

Harlacher, E.L. (1984). No community colleges have not strayed too far from their appropriate missions. *Community and Junior College Journal, 55* (1), 57.

Harlacher, E.L. (1988a). Leadership for a learning society. In E.L.Harlacher (Ed.), *Cutting edge technologies in community colleges*. Washington, D.C.: AACC.

Harlacher, E.L. (1988b). The learning society: a vital role for community services and continuing education. *Community Services Catalyst, 18* (2), 6–8.

Harlacher, E.L. (1992). Building learning communities. *Community College Review, 20* (3), 29–36.

Harlacher, E.L., and Hencey, R.E. Performance-oriented learning: how to do it. In Harlacher, E.L. and Gollattscheck, J.F. (Eds.), *Implementing community-based education*. New Directions for Community Colleges, 21. San Francisco: Jossey-Bass.

Hudgins, J.L. (1990) Renewing a mature community college. *Leadership Abstracts, 3* (4), 1–2.

Joseph, E. (1984). Earl Joseph predicts: training is a growth industry. *Training, 21* (10), 133–135.

Kalamazoo Valley Community College. (1993). *The arcadia commons partnership: the community college and economic redevelopment*. Kalamazoo, MI: author.

Kemp, R.L. (1990). Cities in the year 2000: the forces of change. *The Futurist*, September–October, 13–15.

Knowles, M.S. (1989). Planning for the twenty-first century world. In Norris, N.A. (Ed.), *Community college futures: from rhetoric to reality*. Stillwater, OK: New Forums Press.

Lapin, J.D. (1992). Back to the future: anticipating and preparing for change. *Community College Journal, 63* (1), 29–33.

Lever, J.C. (1992). Meeting increasing demands using distance education. *Leadership Abstracts, 5* (2), 1–2.

Levine, A. (1995). Keynote address at the annual convention of the AACC, Minneapolis, MN.

Lewis, P.H. (1992, June 7). Home is where the office is. *San Jose Mercury News*, p. 1F, 7F.

Lipnack, J. and Stamps, J. (1993). Networking the world. *The Futurist, 27* (4), 9–12.

Lorenzo, A. (1995). *Critical issues facing america's community colleges*. Presentation at the annual convention of the AACC, Minneapolis, MN.

McClenney, K.; LeCroy, N.A.; and LeCroy, J. (1991). *Building communities through strategic planning*. Washington, D.C.: AACC.

McGuire, K.B. (1988). *State of the art in community-based education*. Washington, D.C.: AACC.

Morrison, J.L., and Mecca, T.V. (1990). *The ED QUEST planning model: a process for linking environmental changes with strategic management*. Preconference workshop of the Society for College and University Planning, Atlanta, GA.

Myran, G.A. (1969). *Community services in the community college*. Washington, D.C.: AACC.

Naisbitt, J., and Aburdene, P. (1990). *Megatrends 2000: ten new directions for the 1990's*. New York: William Morrow.

Nanus, B. (1989). *The leader's edge: the seven keys to leadership in a turbulent world*. Chicago: Contemporary Books.

Nickse, R. (1981). *Competency-based education: beyond minimum competency testing*. New York: Teachers College Press.

O'Banion, T. (1993). *Regarding the mission of the community college*. Presentation at the annual convention of the AACC, Portland, Oregon.

Orr, J. (1995). Presentation at the annual conference of the AACC, Minneapolis, MN.

Pedersen, R. (1993). Defining the role of community services. *Community College Week, 6* (4), p. 4.

Phi Delta Kappa. (1984). Handbook for conducting futures studies in education. Bloomington, IN: author.

Puyear, D.E. (1991). An essay: the charrette and long-range planning in the Virginia community college system. *Community College Review, 19* (2), 8–14.

Rockart, J.F. (1979). Chief executives define their own data needs. *Harvard Business Review*, 81–93.

Senge, P.M. (1990). *The fifth discipline: the art and practice of the learning organization*. New York: Doubleday.

Shane, H.G. (1989). Britain's university of the air. *The Futurist*, July–August, 25–27.

Sharples, D.K. (1993). Responding to new workforce realities. *Community College Times, 5* (4), p. 2.

Smith, J.L. (1986). *College centers for older adults*. Washington, D.C.: American Association of Retired Persons.

Steinfels, P. (1992, May 24). A political movement blends its ideas from left and right. *New York Times*.

Szulc, T. (1993, July 25). The greatest danger we face. *Parade*, 4–7.

Tadlock, M.J. (1978). Planning: how to get there. In E. L. Harlacher and J. F. Gollattscheck (Eds.), *Implementing community-based education*, New Directions for Community Colleges, No. 21. San Francisco: Jossey-Bass.

Tate, P. (1995). Presentation at the annual convention of the AACC, Minneapolis, MN.

Toffler, A. (1990). *Powershift*. New York: Bantam Books.

Twigg, C.A. and Doucette, D. (1992). Improving productivity in higher education—a paradigm shift needed. *Leadership Abstracts, 5* (6), 1–2.

Tyree, L.W. (1990). Building communities: the final litmus test. *Community Services Catalyst, 20* (1), 3–5.

Vaughan, G.B. and Gillett-Karam, R. (1993). ACCLAIM: a model for leading the community. *Community College Journal, 63*(6), 20–23.

World Future Society. (1991). The art of forecasting. Bethesda, MD: World Future Society.

Yarrington, R. Assessing the community base. *Community and Junior College Journal,* 1975, 46 (3), p. 7.

Yasuda, G. (1995, March 11, E1). Go to college in your home. *Orlando Sentinel.*

Zeiss, T. (Ed.), (1991). *Creating a literate society: college-business community partnerships.* Washington, D.C.: AACC.

About the Authors

Ervin L. Harlacher is Professor of Higher Education Emeritus at Pepperdine University. During his long and distinguished career he has held the following positions: Chancellor of the Marin Community Colleges, California; Chancellor of the Metropolitan Community Colleges in Kansas City, Missouri; Founding President of Brookdale Community College, New Jersey; Executive Vice President of Oakland Community College in Michigan; and Director of Community Services for the Foothill Community College District in California. Dr. Harlacher is a widely published author in higher education and the community college with a particular emphasis on community services and community-based education. Dr. Harlacher received a B.A. Degree from La Verne College, and his M.A. And Ed.D. degrees from the University of California, Los Angeles.

James F. Gollattscheck has been a teacher or administrator at every level of public education from elementary school through the university. From 1970 to 1984 he was president of Valencia Community College, Florida. From 1984 to 1992 he served as vice president for communications and executive vice president of the American Association of Community Colleges. Since retiring in 1992 he has been actively involving in professional writing and consulting. Dr. Gollattscheck has published several books in addition to a number of journal articles and monographs. Dr. Gollattscheck has been honored with the Lifetime Membership Award from COMBASE. He earned graduate degrees at the University of Florida and Florida State University.